LET'S VISIT...

SCOTLAND

Annabelle Lynch

FRANKLIN WATTS
LONDON · SYDNEY

First published in 2015 by
Franklin Watts
338 Euston Road
London NW1 3BH

Franklin Watts Australia
Level 17/207 Kent Street
Sydney NSW 2000

HB ISBN: 978 1 4451 3701 8
Library eBook: 978 1 4451 3702 5

Dewey classification number:
941.1

Editor: Julia Bird
Designer: Jeni Child
Printed in China

Photo acknowledgements:
Apw/Dreamstime: 7t. Creative Hearts/
Dreamstime: 10b. Viorel Dudau/Dreamstime:
11t. Mark Eastment/Dreamstime: 19t. Ceman
Elias/Alamy: 1, 19b. Fasphotographic/
Dreamstime: 7b. Maria Feklistove/
Dreamstime: 4-5. Nicola Ferrari/Dreamstime:
3bl, 20b. Julie Fryer Images/Alamy: 15t.
Lukas Hejtman/Dreamstime: 16t. Gail
Johnson/Dreamstime: 3br, 4bl, 14t, 15b, 24b.
Anastasiia Kucherenko/Shutterstock: 4tl,
6tl, 8tl, 10tl, 12tl, 14tl, 16tl, 18tl, 20tl. Tamara
Kulikova/Dreamstime: 6b. Charlotte Leaper/
Dreamstime: 2. David Lyons/Alamy: 14b.
Iain Masteron/Alamy: 8b. Daniel Masters/
Dreamstime: 17t. National Geographic/
Alamy: 6t. 10101.101e/Dreamstime: 20tr.
Craig Roberts/Alamy: 18b. Phil Seale/
Alamy: front cover. Neil Setchfield/Alamy:
21b. Claire Shearer/Dreamstime: 9t. Martin
Srubar/Dreamstime: 4br. The Vince 11/
Dreamstime: 11c. Tomzoy/Dreamstime: 8c.
Travel Pictures/Alamy: 5t. Kenny Williamson
Glasgow/Alamy: 21t. Ketsiree Wongwan/
Dreamstime: 12b, 13t, 13b. Adam Woolfit/
Corbis: 17c

Franklin Watts is a division of
Hachette Children's Books,
an Hachette UK company.
www.hachette.co.uk

CONTENTS

Let's Visit Scotland 4

Ben Nevis 6

The Falkirk Wheel 8

Stirling Castle 10

The National Museum 12

The Highland Wildlife Park 14

Skara Brae 16

Isle of Skye 18

Glasgow Science Centre 20

Map of Scotland 21

Glossary 22

Index and Further Information 22

Words in **bold** are in the glossary.

LET'S VISIT
SCOTLAND

Scotland lies to the north of the United Kingdom (UK). It has a long coastline with cliffs and sandy beaches, and is surrounded by lots of islands.

Landscape

In the south of Scotland, there are rolling hills and forests. In the far north, or Highlands, it can be very **mountainous**. In between the two, the land is flatter and good for farming. Most of Scotland's cities, including Edinburgh and Glasgow, are found there.

Red deer live in the Scottish Highlands.

Glasgow is Scotland's biggest city.

When to visit

The weather in Scotland can be different every day! It is usually a little cooler here than in other countries of the UK because it is further north, and it can be a bit wet. The summer is the best time to visit, but it's always worth bringing warm clothes and waterproofs, especially if you are going to be outdoors.

TRAVEL TIP

Scotland is easy to get around. You can travel by car, bus, train, boat or bike!

⬆ It can be warm and sunny in Scotland in summer.

⬆ Scotland has some fine, sandy beaches, such as Sango Bay in the Highlands.

5

BEN NEVIS

You can see for miles from the top of Ben Nevis.

Ben Nevis is the highest mountain in Scotland. About 400,000 people visit it every year and 100,000 of them climb to the top!

King of the Grampians

Ben Nevis is part of the Grampian mountain **range**. The rugged Grampians stretch across the Highlands and have many high mountains.

The top of Ben Nevis is often hidden by clouds.

Top of the world

Ben Nevis stands a mighty 1,344 metres tall. Paths lead all the way up to the **summit**, but it is a long, hard climb! You should wear strong shoes, take plenty of food and water and make sure you keep to the path at all times.

On your way up Ben Nevis, you will pass clear mountain streams.

TRAVEL TIP

The weather on Ben Nevis can change quickly from sunny skies to fog, rain and even snow. Always check the weather forecast before you set off.

 ## Around Ben Nevis

If you can't manage the climb up Ben Nevis, there is still plenty to do nearby. You can go skiing, snowboarding or mountain biking in the mountains around Ben Nevis. Or you can take a **gondola** ride all the way to the top of nearby Aonach Mor.

THREE MORE
MOUNTAINS
TO TACKLE:

Cairn Gorm
Ben Lomond
Ben Macdui

The gondola ride to the top of Aonach Mor takes around 15 minutes.

THE FALKIRK WHEEL

Can you imagine being lifted 35 metres up into the air in a boat, spinning as you go? The Falkirk Wheel does just that!

The Falkirk Wheel is found in central Scotland, in between Edinburgh and Glasgow.

Lift off!

Many great **engineers** come from Scotland, including Thomas Telford who built some of the first **canals**. The Falkirk Wheel is a newer example of engineering. It was built in 2002 to link two canals that run between Edinburgh and Glasgow. It can lift or lower eight boats at a time, moving them between the two waterways.

The Falkirk Wheel uses the same amount of energy to turn as it takes to boil eight kettles!

What to do

You can take your own boat on the wheel, or try ono of the special boat trips. These last for about an hour and take you up and back down in the wheel. Or there are lots of other fun activities to try on a visit here. You can hire canoes, play in the water park, go on a nature trail or just find out all about the wheel in the Visitor Centre.

The Falkirk Wheel is the only boat lift of its kind in the world.

OTHER ENGINEERING MARVELS:

The Forth Bridge
Bell Rock Lighthouse
Caledonian Canal

STIRLING CASTLE

Stirling Castle is one of Scotland's oldest and most important castles. It is perched high on a rocky hill near the old town of Stirling in central Scotland.

Royal home

Stirling Castle has been an important part of Scottish history since the 12th century and many of Scotland's kings and queens were born, crowned and died here. It is found close to a crossing of the River Forth, making it an important **stronghold** for the battles that have been fought here over the years.

Stirling Castle is surrounded on three sides by steep cliffs. It was built on a hill to make it easy to protect.

 Actors bring the **medieval** history of the castle to life.

The grand gatehouse to Stirling Castle.

Find out more

Today, you can explore Stirling Castle for yourself. The Royal Lodgings and magnificent Great Hall show you how the kings and queens lived, while the kitchens and vaults tell you more about the lives of the cooks, musicians and servants who looked after them. Outside the castle, you can walk on the high walls that were built to keep the castle safe from **invaders**.

TRAVEL TIP

Don't miss out on a visit to the palace vaults, where you can dress in medieval costumes and play old musical instruments.

OTHER GREAT **CASTLES:**

Eilean Donan
Cawdor Castle
Edinburgh Castle

THE NATIONAL MUSEUM

When skies are grey, you can head to the National Museum of Scotland in Edinburgh to find out about Scotland – and the world.

 Start your visit to the museum in the beautiful Grand Gallery.

 ## Making the museum

The National Museum of Scotland was formed when two museums joined together in 2006. Parts of the building date back to 1861, others opened as recently as 2011.

TRAVEL TIP

Don't miss the 12-metre-long Tyrannosaurus rex skeleton in the Animal World Gallery!

Play a game with a robot in the Science and Technology collections.

Have a go yourself!

The museum lets you really get involved in its collections. You can dig up a dinosaur's bones, make your own electricity with a wind **turbine**, try on a spacesuit and even drive a model Formula 1 car.

Explore and discover

The museum has more than 20,000 amazing **artefacts** for you to discover, ranging from Ancient Egyptian mummies to Viking chess pieces, and from the first tyre to the famous **cloned** sheep, Dolly.

OTHER **MUSEUMS** TO VISIT:

National Museum of Flight

National War Museum

Glasgow Science Centre (see pages 20–21)

Meet the first-ever cloned sheep, Dolly.

THE HIGHLAND WILDLIFE PARK

Go wild with the animals at the Highland Wildlife Park!

About the park

The Highland Wildlife Park is found in the heart of the Scottish Highlands, close to the town of Aviemore. You can drive around the main reserve in a car, and explore the walk-round area on foot. At different times of day, you can see some of the animals being fed and learn a bit more about them from their keepers.

This Japanese macaque or snow monkey is quite at home in the park.

TRAVEL TIP

If you can't see an animal at first, it's worth coming back for another look later as animals are active at different times of day.

Grey wolves are found in the wild in Europe, but can only be seen in zoos in Britain.

14

Spend some time with the park's polar bears.

OTHER GREAT ZOOS:

Edinburgh Zoo

Blair Drummond Safari Park

Deep Sea World

Meet the animals

You can see animals from all over the world at the Highland Wildlife Park, including rare Scottish wildlife and some **endangered** animals. Make sure you visit the polar bears – they are among the only polar bears found in any British zoo. There are also rare owls, hoofed animals, including elk, bison and reindeer, and four Amur tigers – the biggest tigers in the world.

You can see rare Amur tigers playing in the park.

SKARA BRAE

If you are interested in Scotland's history, Skara Brae on Orkney is a great place to visit.

Skara Brae is found on Mainland, the biggest Orkney island.

OTHER PLACES TO VISIT IN ORKNEY:

Ring of Brodgar
The Old Man of Hoy
Pickaquoy Centre

Uncovering Skara Brae

Skara Brae is the remains of a **Stone Age** village. It is over 5,000 years old. It was discovered during a huge storm in 1850. The strong wind blew away the soil and grass on top of a mound of earth, uncovering some stone houses which had been hidden under the mound for thousands of years.

A house in Skara Brae. The fireplace was in the middle of the room, with space for two beds either side of it. Against the wall was a dresser.

A piece of pottery found in Skara Brae.

The houses

Archaeologists began digging around Skara Brae. They discovered a total of eight houses, linked together by stone passages. Each had four walls, a fireplace, two beds and a stone **dresser**.

TRAVEL TIP

Have a go at making a Stone Age pot at the Visitor Centre.

Find out more

Today, you can explore Skara Brae for yourself. There is a **replica** house which allows you to imagine what life would have been like for the farmers and fishermen who lived in Skara Brae. There is also a visitor's centre where you can see the things found here by archaeologists over the years, such as tools, toys and jewellery.

ISLE OF SKYE

Scotland is surrounded by thousands of islands, both big and small. Some are **inhabited**, but many are not.

TRAVEL TIP

Skye has some of the darkest night skies in Europe, so make sure you do some star-gazing.

Far-flung Skye

Skye is one of Scotland's biggest islands. It is found off the west coast of Scotland in the Inner Hebrides. You can get there on a ferry or by crossing the Skye Bridge.

 The Skye Bridge crosses over the small island of Eilean Bàn.

On the sea

You can spot whales, dolphins and seals off Skye's coast, as wild birds fly overhead. In summer, you can tackle sea kayaking or waterskiing. But wear a wetsuit – the sea is very cold!

Common seals can be spotted on Skye's shores.

Out and about

There are lots of things to do on Skye. You can climb the craggy hills, explore the sandy beaches, go pony trekking or try some real off-road biking!

OTHER **ISLANDS** TO VISIT:

Mull
Harris
Arran

Skye has lots of beautiful beaches to discover.

GLASGOW SCIENCE CENTRE

The Glasgow Science Centre is a fantastic place to have fun learning all about science.

Rebuilding the docks

The Glasgow Science Centre opened in 2001 and is found on the south bank of the River Clyde in Glasgow. This area of **dockland** was once used for shipping, but as the industry fell upon hard times, the dockland was left empty. Today, the Science Centre and new BBC headquarters have brought new life to the area.

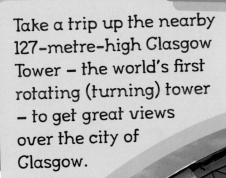

The newly opened Glasgow Tower stands next to the Science Centre.

TRAVEL TIP

Take a trip up the nearby 127-metre-high Glasgow Tower – the world's first rotating (turning) tower – to get great views over the city of Glasgow.

Have a go at some real-life science experiments.

Adventures in science

The Glasgow Science Centre has over 250 amazing science exhibits to discover, from exciting live science experiments to enormous 3-D models of the human body. You can build your own rollercoaster, attempt the bubble wall and take in thousands of twinkling stars in the **planetarium**. If you're tired after all that, you can relax by watching a film at Scotland's first IMAX cinema.

Have fun with the dazzling exhibits in the MindWorks gallery.

OTHER PLACES TO VISIT IN **GLASGOW**:

Botanic Gardens
Pollok Country Park
Scottish Football Museum

The Science Centre building was designed to look like the hull (body) of a ship.

MAP OF SCOTLAND

N

6

7

5

1

GRAMPIANS

3

GLASGOW

EDINBURGH

8

2

4

KEY:
- 1 Ben Nevis
- 2 The Falkirk Wheel
- 3 Stirling Castle
- 4 The National Museum
- 5 The Highland Wildlife Park
- 6 Skara Brae
- 7 Isle of Skye
- 8 Glasgow Science Centre

GLOSSARY

archaeologist
Someone who digs up objects to find out about the past

artefact
An object, such as a piece of jewellery, which has been made by men, not by machine

canal
A narrow, man-made stretch of water

cloned
An exact copy of something else

dockland
The area around ship docks

dresser
A piece of furniture with shelves and cupboards

endangered
At risk of dying out

engineer
Someone who designs and helps to build buildings and other structures, such as roads

gondola
A cabin that is carried on a cable through the air

inhabited
Lived in

invader
Someone who enters a place by force and takes it over

medieval
From a period of history called the Middle Ages. This lasted from around the 5th to the 15th centuries CE

mountainous
An area where there are lots of mountains

planetarium
A big room in which the planets and stars are shown on a rounded ceiling

range
A group of mountains

replica
A copy of something

Stone Age
A period of time when man learned to use stone tools. In the British Isles it lasted from the end of the last Ice Age, about 10,000 years ago, until the Bronze Age, about 4,500 years ago

stronghold
A place that is easy to defend

summit
The top

turbine
A machine that uses the power of air or water to turn a wheel and produce energy

INDEX

beaches 4, 5, 19
Ben Nevis 6–7, 22

canals 8–9
castles 10–11

Edinburgh 4, 8, 11–13
engineering 8–9

Falkirk Wheel 8–9, 22

Glasgow 4, 8, 20–21

Glasgow Science Centre 13, 20–22

Highland Wildlife Park 14–15, 22
Highlands 4–7, 14–15

islands 4, 16–19
Isle of Skye 18–19, 22

landscape 4–5

map 22

mountains 4, 6–7

National Museum 12–13, 22

Skara Brae 16–17, 22
Stirling Castle 10–11, 22

transport 5

weather 5, 7
wildlife 4, 14–15, 19

FURTHER INFORMATION

Books

Fact Cat: Scotland by Alice Harman (Wayland, 2014)

Living in the UK: Scotland by Annabelle Lynch (Franklin Watts, 2014)

Websites

www.visitscotland.com

www.bbc.co.uk/scotland/learning/primary/skarabrae/

www.nms.ac.uk/explore/play/

Every effort has been made by the Publishers to ensure that the websites are suitable for children, and that they contain no inappropriate or offensive material. However, because of the nature of the Internet, it is impossible to guarantee that the contents of these sites will not be altered. We strongly advise that Internet access is supervised by a responsible adult.